YOU BECOME WHAT YOU THINK ABOUT

How your mind creates
the world you live in

VIC JOHNSON

Laurenzana Press

Published by:

Laurenzana Press

PO Box 1220

Melrose, FL 32666 USA

www.LaurenzanaPress.com

****

ISBN-13: 978-1-937918-81-1

TABLE OF CONTENTS

Introduction

THINKING WITH MIND AND HEART

"As a man thinketh in his heart, so is he" is one of the most powerful statements known to man. In fact, James Allen (the famous self-help author) made it the hallmark of his classic masterpiece, *As a Man Thinketh* (get a free copy at www.AsAManThinketh.net.)

You may not know the true implication of those words from the Book of Proverbs (23:7). For example, in ancient Greek the word "heart" didn't mean the physical organ, but rather referred to the unconscious or subconscious mind.

Others have expressed the same idea with different words. Buddha, for example, declared that, "The mind is everything. What you think you become." "You become what you think about all day long" is how Ralph Waldo Emerson expressed it.

I was first exposed to the idea in a recording by

Earl Nightingale called *The Strangest Secret;* which became the only personal development recording ever to receive a Gold Record.

What is the strangest secret? "You become what you think about," said Nightingale.

When those words really came home to me my life was upside down. My family and I had been evicted from our home and lost our last automobile to repossession. I earned so little money during that time that we qualified below the U.S. poverty level for a family of five.

At first I rejected the idea that "you become what you think about" because it would mean that I was responsible for our miserable condition. But the more I studied and the more I thought about it, the more sense it made to me that if my thinking had gotten me in the mess I was in, then my thinking could also be my savior and lead me to a better life.

Is it true that we can trace our beliefs, actions, doubts or decisions to our subconscious thoughts? Doesn't everything we do ultimately spring forth from the way we think?

If you've ever stopped taking a certain action because something in your "heart" told you it was wrong, you experienced the effect subconscious thinking has on your actions and by extension your circumstances.

Everyone has a conscious mind capable of making a variety of decisions on a day-to-day basis. But many of them are not decisions, but rather actions you take as a result of habit. For many people, their biggest daily decision can be whether or not to take the scenic or same route to work, or whether to part their hair on the left instead of the right. Therefore, it's subconscious versus conscious habits that can affect real change on your life.

Your subconscious mind is responsible for just about every major thing in your life. You don't have to consciously think about breathing, your heart beating, walking, or how to properly digest and metabolize the food you eat.

A deeply embedded, ancient part of you handles all of that work, and therein lies the wisdom of *"As a man thinketh in his heart, so is he."*

Effecting Change

Without the cooperation of your subconscious—the deep recesses of your inner self—change can be difficult to impossible. You might consciously have tried to lose weight. But if your subconscious mind was fixated on fattening food and how difficult exercise was, the experience was probably a challenge or a dismal failure. Therefore, changing one or more aspects of your life can't occur until you affect change on your subconscious.

To try and change your life through conscious thought is similar to expecting an orchard to grow by throwing apples on the ground and hoping a tree will grow. But a wise person will clear the land of weeds, till the soil, fertilize the ground, plant the seeds, water them every day, and keep the soil free of weeds as the tree grows.

Your subconscious is the farm that will produce well if you plant thoughts (the seeds) and cultivate the fertile soil you need in order to grow as a person. Your conscious mind is the "farmer" that is ultimately responsible for caretaking your farm.

You're responsible for your own mental destiny that will determine where you end up and ultimately who you become. So let's take a closer look at how to change your thoughts that will allow you to lead a life you love.

(**Attention All Eagle Eyes**: We've had a number of people proof this book before we released it to you, but there is a chance you might spot something that was missed. If you find a typo or other obvious error, please send it to us. And if you're the first one to report it <u>we'll send you a free gift</u>! Send to: corrections@laurenzanapress.com)

CHAPTER ONE
CAUSE AND EFFECT

Sir Isaac Newton, one of the greatest physicists and thinkers of all time, said "For every action there is an equal and opposite reaction." In other words, for every effect there is a cause, and for every cause there is an effect.

You may already be familiar with the concept of cause and effect. But when was the last time (if ever) you took a step back and viewed your life from this perspective? Maybe you believe everything that happens (especially negative things) is the effect of some external cause. You might think, *I wouldn't have so much stress at work if my boss would treat me better.*

However, what would happen if you saw yourself *as* the cause of all the effects in your life? For example, what if your *reactions* to your work environment were the true cause of your stress?

If you choose to look at it this way, you might have to face some harsh truths about yourself.

On the flip side, there's a certain freedom that comes with this kind of realization. Because if you can cause negative effects in your life, you can cause better, more positive effects (what a concept)! This puts you in the driver's seat, and once you learn how to be in control of your steering it's a very good place to be!

Five Common Causes That Lead to Disempowering Effects

Many common problems can be traced back to small, subtle causes that led to the problems (the effects) in the first place. Take a look at five of these common causes, and see if you can identify with any of them:

1. Living Life Reactively Instead of Proactively

The first mistake many people make is they readily give power over to disempowering thoughts, circumstances, obstacles, and external settings that negatively affect them. Of course, there's negativity in the world beyond your control, and real obstacles do exist. But in and of themselves, obstacles hold no real power over you unless you choose to give them power.

For example, how many times have you listened to someone who said they wanted to accomplish something but couldn't because of one particular obstacle or excuse? "I'd like to write my book, but I don't know anyone in publishing." Or "I really want to take tango lessons, but it's hard to find a babysitter."

You want to say, "Oh, for heaven's sake! There are books, websites and hundreds of people who can help you find the right publisher." Or, "That's easy. Make a list of people who might have a suggestion of a babysitter, and collect names so you always have one available." Therefore, the only real obstacle to achievement is your subconscious working against your conscious mind.

The power of obstacles is drawn from the same power we all possess to make things happen. The question is whether or not you'll surrender to negative power, or claim the power of strength to overcome your obstacles.

Look at the circumstances around you as malleable clay. You may not like how life has taken shape, but that doesn't mean it won't change if you mold it into the "sculpture" you've envisioned it to be.

2. Giving Other People Control

When you give other people power over your life, they might pick some causes that won't lead you to your goals and dreams.

Sadly, many people measure their self-esteem by

other people's opinions. They worry too much about what their colleagues think of them, whether or not they might get rejected if they ask someone out on a date, or try to manipulate situations so they can look better than they actually do. The problem with these kinds of actions is they're the effects of skewed thoughts (the cause) and the lack of self-confidence.

Losing power ultimately gives people control over your decisions. If you hold the subconscious attitude that your self-worth is measured by others, you give people the power to harshly judge you. As a consequence you become stifled, worried, and anxious about how they view you. Your actions stem from these badly twisted thoughts, and the results aren't very pretty.

So don't give people control over how you think and the decisions you make. Instead, take control of yourself and your power as it was originally meant to be.

3. Giving Up Too Easily

When people hear about the power of thought, they often think about it as "one single thought" which can be very limiting. True, a single thought doesn't have much power if it's fighting against an entire sea of thoughts. But that doesn't mean the power of thought should be quickly tossed aside and dismissed.

Many people give up too easily because they don't understand that subconscious thought changes as a result of sustained thought and action. For instance, a salesman starting a new job wouldn't quit after failing one sales pitch. To that end, why would anyone trying something new quit after only one or a few unsuccessful attempts?

It's in failure where you learn more about yourself, grow new habits, change strategies, and learn how not to fail at your goals. Failure is a very useful tool as it helps to shape your thoughts more efficiently and more logically. Giving up simply because you're failing suggests failure itself contains the power, rather than the successful thinking that occurs because of what you learn by failing. Therefore, giving up is another form of giving your power away; only this time, you give it away to failure which is no way to live.

James Allen said it takes "a lot of mining to find the gold." You'll find success only after you've searched for it more than anyone else. If you expect instant success, you probably won't see rewards for your efforts. The process of expecting success is what will help you develop a healthy attitude towards persistence.

4. Focusing on Lack Instead of Abundance

There's a lot of power in focusing on lack or abundance. For instance, changing the angle of glass can shift sunlight from a relatively harmless warm ray into an intensified beam that is–powerful enough to start fires.

It can be a constant struggle to see a glass as half full rather than half empty. Focusing on the lack of success in your life rather than the abundance of success gives more power to the emptiness of your "glass." But focusing on an abundance of success fills the "glass" to overflowing!

There's always something positive to be found in every situation. If you only have $500 in your bank account, consider all the people who are millions of dollars in debt. If you're struggling to lose weight, consider all the people who don't have enough to eat.

There is always something to be grateful for, and you can find power, happiness and positivity in gratitude. So don't give power to what's missing in your life, but what is evident and abundant, and you'll fill your "glass" quickly and with substance.

5. Failing to Find the "Polar Opposites" in Life

Just about everything in life has an opposite: Darkness and light, ups and downs, loud and quiet, happy and sad. Life's challenges also have their opposites.

Say you have a flat tire on the way to work, so you first identify what's wrong with the tire (a nail, lost its tread because it's old, etc.). You're likely going to have to pay money for a new tire, and you're going to be late to work. You might have to rely on someone driving by to change the tire for you (which can be embarrassing), and you may have to drive to the gas station or work on a spare tire. You've lost many hours dealing with this problem, so you end up tired and cranky and backlogged at work or with running errands.

But if everything has a polar opposite, there must be something good about getting a flat tire. For example, when you go in later to buy a new tire, the dealer will make a sale which will help them pay their bills. When they're checking to see what kind of tire you need, they notice something about your car that needs to be fixed. And by fixing it ahead of time you might save hundreds of dollars down the road that didn't cost as much now. Maybe you had to wait around for the tire to be fixed, which helped you de-stress while reading a book. Or if you didn't know how to fix a tire before, and you do now!

Have you ever seen someone lose their job or get left by a spouse, only to say "It was the best thing that happened to me"? If so, you've witnessed someone who can find the opposites—and the opportunities—in every situation.

This happened in my own life. In 1999 I had the opportunity to create an Internet venture, and was promised some pretty significant things by some pretty significant people. So I dropped what I was doing to undertake this project, even though I couldn't afford to spend the time and money it required.

But because there was so much potential in this opportunity, I decided to give it a try. Then after all the work I put into developing the product and people's promises hadn't been kept, I lost time and investment money on something that went nowhere, and I lost income I needed to pay bills.

Now, I'm not one to say a positive mental attitude trumps everything, because this event in my life caused some pretty big heartaches. But years later after I finally did have profitable Internet ventures, I realized all of my success had been planted by that first failure. My time and effort I thought I had wasted eventually paid great dividends, even if they weren't what I had hoped for initially.

This isn't to say you won't have regrets. But sometimes it's important to recognize that even when you try and fail, you still can build towards a better future.

Finding the Causes of Your Life's Effects

Now that you know five of the most common ways people surrender power through their thoughts, it's time to identify ways you can constructively shape the causes and effects in your life.

We're not going to start with the causes, but rather diagnose what's wrong by identifying the effects. Why? Because effects are the most obvious. And since every effect has a cause, it would be beneficial to use the obvious effects to identify some not-so-obvious causes.

Unhappiness

The topic of "how to be happy" could fill several volumes of books. Heck, it could fill an entire library, and you still wouldn't know everything on the subject of happiness versus unhappiness.

At the core of unhappiness or happiness is thought. How many things in your past can you identify as being negative? Undoubtedly, there were some events that had little redeeming value, so you were better off without them.

But if you dig deep enough you'll find events that seemed negative at the time, but turned out to be positive in terms of your overall growth and long-term happiness.

You can't always control your circumstances, but you can choose to be happy. When you're unhappy it's not the result of circumstances but the result of thought, which is why feeling unhappy often coincides with feelings of helplessness. To be happy is associated with the knowledge that how you think and feel will always be your choice, which will put you in charge of your life.

Automatic Negativity

You're not alone if you say "I always try to be positive, but it doesn't work!" whenever you read or talk about positive thinking. Many people who want to think more positively struggle to change their ways. But through willpower alone they eventually settle back into old habits, which is a symptom of the under-lying cause of automatic (or conditioned) negativity.

If you've been creating negative thought patterns for a long time, it's going to be difficult to toss them aside overnight. However, conditioned negativity doesn't have to be the end of the world. If you want to change the flow of a river you wouldn't do it over-night; you'd start small, and slowly build the founda-tion for changing the river's flow.

At first you can make small, adaptable changes to the flow of your thoughts. Then as you exercise your newfound ability to selectively choose your thoughts, you'll eventually become better at larger changes.

The Blame Game

If you're the kind of person who thinks *if it weren't for so-and-so*, or *if I could just get X and Y out of my life, then I could...*, you need to stop playing the blame game. Blaming yourself is an effect of not empower-ing yourself with responsibility for your own life. The faster you accept responsibility for your current situ-ation and your thoughts, the better off you'll be.

The reason the blame game never works (aside from the fact it irritates others) is that by blaming someone else for your misfortune you give them the power to bring you misfortune. This isn't an empow-ering mindset; it's the cause of disastrous effects the blame game can have on your life. So you're going to have to shift your focus if you want to change it.

END OF CHAPTER ASSIGNMENT

You're to identify one negative thought or self-perception that has brought about the circumstances in which you find yourself (which shouldn't be difficult to identify. In fact, the answer might jump out at you and take you by surprise.)

For instance, think about someone who thinks of and describes themselves as clumsy. Their suspicions are confirmed every time they bump their knee on a coffee table or spill a glass of milk.

Give this some thought and write it down. Then in the next chapter I'm going to show you how you can change your perception to alter your circumstances.

CHAPTER TWO

PLANTING NEW SEEDS

"You reap what you sow" is timeless wisdom. Yet how many people apply it to their ordinary day-to-day lives on a regular basis?

In the previous chapter on cause and effect you learned that your circumstances often happen as a result of your thoughts. In other words, you're reaping the harvest of thoughts you've been sowing all your life.

It stands to reason that if you want new effects, you're going to have to change the causes. If you want to watch the fruit of your efforts grow, you're going to have to plant different kinds of seeds. Nature has a consistent pattern of planting seeds, germination, and growth, which is why if you want to change anything you have to start at the "seed" or "soil" level.

You don't see apple seeds sprouting into wine vineyards, or pumpkin seeds growing into mango trees. Instead, everything grows from its own particular nature. Even if you were to try to change an apple orchard into a vineyard by cutting down the trees and planting grapevines, would the vines actually grow if the soil wasn't fertile? Or would the field itself change according to what's planted in the soil?

It's the same with your thoughts. But changing your thoughts isn't as easy as it seems; in fact, many people are so conditioned to think in a certain way that they have trouble identifying where to begin. So let's start from the outside and work our way back in to see how your thoughts are affecting your life.

Controlling the Flow of Information: Filtering "External" Thoughts

The stimuli you encounter on a daily basis can be considered a form of "external" thought. Don't believe it? Consider this: Have you ever felt depressed after reading bad news in the newspaper? Have you changed your world view based on what you see on the nightly news? Do you find yourself changing your attitudes and beliefs in order to fit in with the people in your life because you want them to like you?

There's no power like internal thought, but that doesn't mean "external thoughts" won't have a powerful effect on the way you think. If you're going to plant new or different seeds of thought, you're going to have to change the stimuli that make you feel bad and think negatively.

For starters, let's consider the different sources of "external" thoughts that filter into your reality on a daily basis:

> **News:** I've taken many steps to reduce the impact news has on the way my mind works. In fact, a friend publishes our hometown newspaper and I don't subscribe to it. Cutting myself off from most media outlets—many of which are designed to get you to think a certain way—has been an important part in changing my "thought conditioning."

> **Social Influences:** There's an old adage that you become the average of your five closest friends. In fact, some scientists think that some non-contagious conditions, like obesity, are "socially contagious," which is why it's really important to monitor your friends, what they add to your life, and be very careful about who you spend your time with.

> **Entertainment:** You may have heard the expression "mindless entertainment." But because entertainment has an impact on what's going on in your mind, there really is no such thing as it all has a good or bad impact on your mind. Do you seek out enter-

tainment that stimulates your intellect, challenges your assumptions, and builds your confidence? Or do you look for the lowest common denominator because it doesn't force you to think?

You can evaluate whether these kinds of stimuli are helping you by asking yourself *if I eliminate X from my life, will I be better for it?* In many cases, the answer is a simple "yes."

Don't Plant Seeds Until You Know What You Want to Grow

Both James Allen and the New Testament often incorporate the metaphor of "fruit," which is quite apropos to planting the right seeds in the right soil, nurturing the seeds, and allowing them to grow into a tree that bears delectable fruit.

But before we discuss how to nurture your internal thoughts, let's start with the goal of producing tasty "fruit." You need to first ask yourself what do you want your thoughts to produce? And what kind of life do you want to lead?

Although many people have a vague idea about what they want, it works better to get very specific. After all, you're not going to grow succulent oranges unless you know specifically how to grow them.

And what works best for apples won't work best for oranges.

So start with the end in mind. What kind of fruit you want your thoughts to bear is a very important question to ask. James Allen echoed the New Testament when he said, "He that seeketh findeth. And to him that knocketh it shall be opened." (Matthew 7:8)

What does this mean? Well, like most thoughts of wisdom it can mean many different things. But one thing for sure is specificity is crucial because you want to knock on the right door.

We often use the power of our thoughts to create circumstances we don't want. We worry, fret, beat ourselves up, and then are surprised when we don't get what we think we wanted. But now we can open the door we've been knocking on, and pick the fruit we planted a long time ago.

So once again, begin with the end in mind, because having the answer first is not only easier but will help you develop the right questions. Start with your goals and think about what kind of life you really want to create. From there, it's only a matter of cultivating your thoughts and actions to align with those goals.

Taking Charge of the Soil

James Allen said, "Act is the blossom of thought, and joy and suffering are its fruit. Thus does a man garner in the sweet and bitter fruitage of his own husbandry."

You might not know it, but when you were born you were essentially given "land" on which to cultivate your mind. Over the years people have influenced what you should grow there, such as negative and/or positive thoughts. But ultimately, no matter what you do, that acreage will always be there as it's inherently the core of who you are. And going forward you'll be in control of what you will allow to be planted there.

Many people decide to ignore this simple fact and stumble through life. Or they may have goals, but only act on them when they have to. They never really take the time to change the way they think, which at times can be a good thing because after all, the actions you take can affect a lot of changes on your thoughts and vice versa. But if you really want to take charge of the soil, you're going to have to do both.

So how do you take charge of your own soil? Simple. By planting seeds of thoughts. In the previous chapter you were to think about what you want out of life. Now it's time to list the thoughts and attitudes that will eventually take you there.

Give your subconscious mind "orders":
Napoleon Hill, author of *Think and Grow
Rich*, believed in giving your subconscious
mind orders in a very direct way, usually
through the use of affirmations. Be as direct
as you want. Wake up every morning and
say firmly "I'm going to be happy today!" (Or
utilize the thoughts and attitudes you just
read about in the section on "planting seeds.")

Prepare the soil: You can't plant seeds
in stones and sand and expect to see much
growth – if at all. So you need to prepare your
environment – your "swath of land"—for your
new thoughts and affirmations. But this isn't
just about picking "weeds" from your soil; it's
about replacing the soil with something newer
and more fertile.

Think about James Allen's quote "As a man thinketh in his heart, so is he." Many people might tackle
only one or two strategies listed above without incorporating all of them, which will result in incomplete
seed germination.

For example, you know that doing bicep curls can
help get you in shape. So you decide to do a lot of them
every day to help you get lean, fit, and healthy. Well,
even though bicep curls work, it doesn't mean they're
going to get you completely healthy without incorporating other components such as eating nutritious

food, getting enough sleep, eliminating stress, etc. You may have planted the seed for fitness by starting the bicep curls, but you haven't really sowed the seeds of success by preparing the soil with everything you need to get and keep you healthy.

You're Always Planting Seeds

If someone tells you not to think of a pink elephant, guess what you picture in your mind? A pink elephant! Which is why it's impossible not to be planting seeds on your farm. If you want to change your life, you simply have to change how your mind sees the seeds.

Previous sections discussed how to remove bad influences and negative thoughts from your mindset and attitude. But it's not a complete strategy as you have to have replacements for those influences.

For example, many people who give up junk food will start biting their nails. Physically it's an improvement, but it's not the healthiest way to deal with stress or anxiety (and will lead to unsightly hands!). But finding new influences to replace outdated, ineffective ones is easier said than done. For instance, if you cut a friend out of your life, it's not always easy to find a new one.

Finding new positive influences will require getting out of your comfort zone. For example, if your previous after-work routine was to eat a microwave dinner while vegging in front of the TV, you may want to replace that time with an hour at the gym. Although it's not an easy replacement as it takes effort, it eventually will become a part of your routine, and you'll enjoy it even more because of how good you'll feel.

Or you might replace your weekend entertainment with volunteering, taking hikes up big hills, or anything that gets you out of the house. You may join your local theater troupe or take an improv class. By seeking more stimulating activities, you'll come into contact with like-minded people who can be a more positive influence on your life than you ever imagined.

Stop Looking for Outside Help

If you're familiar with the "acres of diamonds" story, you already know the importance of looking inside yourself first to solve your problems. But for those of you who haven't heard it, there was a farmer who had a lust for diamonds, so he sold his farm and went on a search around the world to find diamonds. The search eventually bankrupted him and he was penniless when he died. Guess what the people who bought the farm found on the acreage? Yep, you got it. Diamonds!

This story illustrates the importance of looking within for answers before you look for external sources. If your thoughts are the seeds through which you grow your success, then how on earth can you expect to find success anywhere else but inside yourself?

You empower yourself when you stop looking for help outside, because you give power to your thoughts rather than to the outside world. You can stop relying on other people's opinions to validate your self-confidence and self-esteem. And the only questions you need answers for are the ones you ask yourself.

There's an old saying that if you want to make friends you must first be a friend, and you can practice by being a friend to yourself. If you can learn to be comfortable with yourself, chances are people will also be comfortable in your company, which is a less selfish way to view the world.

When you focus on what you can bring to the table, you stop worrying about what you can get from others. But when people can sense your need for validation and lack of fulfillment, they will feel uncomfortable around you because they worry you'll suck out their energy (called "emotional vampirism"). However, when you feel self-validated and confident, they will seek you out because they know there's no hidden agenda (and no energy sucking), and they enjoy your company.

The comedic actor Jim Carrey once said he wished everyone could have the money and fame he had so they would find out—as he had—that it wasn't the answer to happiness. If someone who's achieved the same level of success he has can say that, what does that mean about seeking the answers outside yourself instead of within?

Do you really think winning the lottery or earning

the respect of your colleagues will make your life better? When you're on your deathbed will you say, "I'm so glad I got people to like me"? Absolutely not! The only thing that matters is the self-perception you'll carry with you for your entire life.

Forget the Notion of a "Future"

People put way too much emphasis on the future. Of course, it's good to save money for your children's college fund. Or to work towards a goal that isn't immediately tangible but might appear somewhere down the road.

But too many people make the future a crutch. You see, when we think about the future we generally don't associate the emotions of the present with it. We think, *I can start that diet on Monday, and I'll be really strict!* But when Monday arrives we realize it's just another "today" and it's just as hard to start, so we put it off for another day (or another Monday).

If you've ever seen the film "Rocky III" you know Rocky's trainer is his old nemesis, Apollo Creed. Rocky (Sylvester Stallone) struggles with feelings of inadequacy—as if the training he's doing is pointless. During one sparring session he tells Apollo he'll try harder "tomorrow." Creed angrily shouts, "There is no tomorrow!" It may sound cliché, but "tomorrow never comes" is very true as we live life in a series of todays.

You're never going to build skills, wealth, and success if you keep putting them off. In essence, thinking about tomorrow gives power to something outside yourself. If you want to do good things in your life, you have to start today.

Procrastinating only puts off an inevitable failure; but taking immediate action will set the course for success, which is a critical lesson to learn, because many people—even those who consider themselves big-time dreamers—allow the future to elude them. "One day…" they keep telling themselves, "one day I'll do better." But that day never comes.

Therefore, there is no tomorrow. There is no outside. There are only the seeds you plant today here and now on your own swath of land.

END OF CHAPTER ASSIGNMENT

In the previous chapter assignment you examined a belief you have about yourself. Now, after knowing what you learned in this chapter, you need to take it a step further by asking yourself what kind of seed you can plant today that would fly in the face of that perception.

In short, you need to create a new empowering affirmation that builds your confidence, which should be the opposite of your previously held belief. For example, if the belief is "I am clumsy," you can overcome it with a positive affirmation such as "I am well-coordinated and graceful."

Remember, there are no negative thoughts, so just saying "I am not clumsy" won't help. It will only have you focusing on how clumsy you think you are the same way "I am not thinking about a pink elephant" gets you thinking about a pink elephant.

Let's try another example. If you have a belief such as "others are more talented than me," you could change it to an empowering thought like "I am talented" or "I like the talents I have" or "I really like the way I sing."

Saying affirmations might feel a little awkward until you get used to incorporating them into your life and begin to feel their effects. One particular affirmation may not change your life, but you can find one (or more) that will resonate with you through trial and effort.

Since this chapter was all about planting seeds, you're planting a seed that through good soil and effective nurturing will eventually grow into an internal belief that will change your external actions.

Get it? Great! So now we'll move on to turn your thoughts into action.

CHAPTER THREE

THE ROLE OF ACTION

James Allen wrote "Good thoughts and actions can never produce bad results; bad thoughts and actions can never produce good results."

It's interesting that he used "thoughts and actions" since he said "As a man thinketh in his heart, so is he." Apparently he recognized that thought independent of action was not enough to bring about change to people's lives. He also knew we can't get very far if our actions don't correspond to our thoughts.

How many people have thought about making changes in their lives, only to see those changes never get made because they didn't see the value in taking action? Yes, you are what you think. But without taking action, you might as well sit in a cave and think about the life you could be living instead of living it.

Your thoughts are meant to inspire and interact

with the world around you. Therefore, if your thoughts are the seeds, your actions are the first sprouting buds that break out of the soil and into sunlight.

Action: Applied Thought

In a sense, action can be thought of as "applied thought." Although action is different than thought it's not entirely separate, because actions influence our thoughts and our thoughts influence our actions. The two have an interdependent relationship that can't be ignored if you want to find more success for yourself.

It's true that if you change your thoughts your actions will also change. But did you know your thoughts also respond to your actions, and that science has proven that smiling produces feelings (and thoughts) of happiness?

This means it's entirely possible to reverse engineer your thoughts by first taking action.

That's not to say you should have one without the other; it's just to demonstrate that both are powerful ways of changing your circumstances. By understanding this premise, you can begin to utilize the full power of the tools you have at your disposal.

Actions are the "fruits" of thought. In the Bible the New Testament talks about how you can know someone's thoughts by witnessing the fruits of their spirit. One major aspect of these "fruits" are the actions they take.

For example, you might feel like a charitable person, but how charitable are you without actions to back up those feelings? Are you really giving with your time and your money? Or do you go through the motions by writing a check once in a while just to appease your guilt?

James Allen wrote "good thoughts and actions can never produce bad results" most likely because thoughts and actions are so closely intertwined into our reality that it's impossible to separate them, which is why action—when thought of as applied thought—is such an important piece of the puzzle.

For example, it's impossible to feel self-conscious when your thoughts and actions are in alignment with "I feel confident." If you puff your chest out, give people solid eye contact, and think confident thoughts, it's virtually impossible to feel self-conscious if you're truly in alignment.

It's when either your thoughts or your actions (or possibly both) are out of alignment that this fails. For example, let's say you've started doing affirmations for a few minutes every morning and at night, which is great! But if your actions throughout the day reinforce a different reality, it's going to be difficult for those affirmations to truly work. There are many hours between morning and night, and how you spend those hours matters.

So thinking of action as "thoughts made physical" can make you more mindful of the actions you take on a daily basis. You can learn to develop an alignment between how you want to feel and how you want to behave, but you have to take action to make it happen.

Actions Only Take Place in the Present

This might sound like an odd thing to say, but your subconscious mind has a sort of timelessness to it as it's always at work, even when you sleep. Subconscious thoughts are expressed during dreams and throughout the day as if they're some sort of time machine.

However, actions are different because they're not static. You can't treat them as you would your subconscious thoughts (because they're not exactly the same thing), which can be a problem for many people since taking action creates fear and anxiety.

Let's say you're interested in getting in shape, only you don't like running because you feel pain in your side and exhaustion in your lungs. So you end up grabbing a soda and lie on the couch to watch television, or go arrange your underwear drawer, or putter around in the garage.

You know running is good for you, and that it's in alignment with the thought *I am healthy*. Yet when it comes right down to the nitty-gritty of actually accomplishing this single action, you think of ways to avoid it.

One way to help the situation is to realize that

actions can only take place in the present. Procrastination is simply a way of deceiving yourself into believing your actions will be easier in the future.

Is that really true? It might be easier to go to the gym at 5:00 p.m. than it is at 5:00 a.m. because you're more awake and less inclined to go back to bed. But don't be surprised if going to the gym feels hard any time of the day because an action is an action is an action. Period.

Using willpower to see an action through is possible, but it's not an ideal solution because many people aren't very good at it. Research has suggested that willpower is like anything else. Although we can get better at it the more we use it, we have limited amounts available. If you tax your system all day through stress at work, and drag yourself out of bed each morning, then how easy do you think it would be to get yourself to the gym?

What is action, after all, if not making things different than they really are? It's comfortable to keep things the way they are, so you've got to get used to the idea of experiencing discomfort.

You can start slowly. Many people recommend taking cold showers, for example, because they not only help wake you up but get you used to feeling uncomfortable. When you start your day with a cold shower, you realize that starting work isn't as stressful as it once was. After all, you just endured five minutes of ice cold water on your skin, so anything else is a breeze.

What you don't want to do is forget that action always takes place in the present. Sometimes it hurts and sometimes it makes you nervous. But as James Allen said, "Suffering is always the effect of wrong thought in some direction."

There's a difference between having a difficult run out of self-love or true suffering. After the run you'll feel invigorated and healthy, but is that real suffering? No, it isn't – it's stimulating. Instead, you can use the pain associated with action to alleviate suffering in your life.

Habits: The "Subconscious" Aspect of Actions

Although your actions are distinctly different from your thoughts, you'd be surprised at the degree to which they connect. This is especially true if you're talking about habits, which are a form of "active thought."

Your habits are formed in your subconscious mind. In fact, that very fact makes it hard to identify the bad habits you already have as some are downright invisible. For example, let's say you have a habit of getting home from work and opening a can of soda. As you're drinking the soda you get the urge for junk food, so before you know it you're reaching for a bag of chips.

But on a different day you watch an important

sports game and forget about the soda. Then hours later, you realize you didn't grab the bag of chips either. So are the two habits interconnected?

Habits are like a river. The Colorado River is a wide stream of water that over millions of years, and with unceasing action, carved out the Grand Canyon. This is why it can be difficult to replace old habits, because like the Colorado River they've carved deep grooves in your life. Changing the flow of the river requires a lot of work, but once you establish new habits the flow will work for you and not against you.

If your commute is 20 or 30 minutes one way every day, it gives you 40 to 60 minutes of free time in your car 250 days out of the year. Simply changing the morning talk show to something more constructive like motivational or language learning CDs can leave you in a completely different place by the end of the year. Therefore, little changes can mean big results over time.

If you want to change your habits, I'd like to suggest following these three tips:

1. **Take time to examine the habits you currently have.** Get out a piece of paper and a pen (or your laptop), and in as much detail as possible put down what a typical day looks like. What processes follow each other? When you read the repetitive order in which you accomplish your daily actions, you might be surprised at some habits you weren't aware of.

2. **Identify some places in your day where you have "empty time."** One example is the commute to work; another might be your lunch break. Finding time that can be stimulating rather than merely entertaining is an opportunity for further growth.

3. **Create a list of substitutes for those habits.** Don't try to change too much about your day, but tweak a few things here and there. Do you cook breakfast every day? Maybe you can use that same time to prepare a healthy lunch as well since your time is already spent cooking.

There's more value than you might realize in each little tweak. Changing your habits on a daily basis might not seem like a lot of change for the first few days, but over the course of weeks, months and even years, the changes can mean a great deal of difference to your life.

New Actions Make New Thoughts

Have you ever had an experience that changed the way you thought about the world? Have you ever read a book that made you think differently about how to approach a problem? If so, you know the power actions have to change the way you think.

The idea here is taking action is more powerful than the experience (taking action generates the experience). For example, you may have thought "I'm not attractive," then someone gives you a compliment that says otherwise. But if you keep thinking *I'm not attractive*, the person's compliment won't have any effect on how you perceive yourself.

You might feel good for a while, but eventually your old belief will resurface. You might rationalize your experience by thinking, *they might have been playing a trick on me*, or *that's just one person—everyone else thinks I'm unattractive*. In that case your thoughts dominate the reality of your experience, which is an example of how negative thoughts about yourself can cause you to experience more pain than necessary.

But if you take action toward becoming more attractive, you create more and more opportunities to prove you are indeed attractive. Let's say you start eating healthier food, working out, and buy stylish clothes that fit you perfectly. Not only will you have spent time taking action, but you'll look better thanks to all your hard work. Then all this incontrovertible evidence shows up in the mirror, and you feel attractive!

Your new way of thinking reflects the new reality as dictated by your actions. In essence, when you do good you start to feel good, even if the process is uncomfortable at first. This is just one example of how you can "hack" into your mind to create more productive thoughts. Here are some of my favorite ways to make sure I continue to cultivate positive thoughts:

Reading: Reading is essentially "injecting" thoughts straight into the bloodstream as it's a very direct way of exercising your mind. What you read has more of an effect than you realize (i.e., a recent study found that reading literary fiction can make you more perceptive), so you should carefully choose your reading material. It's recommended that you spend at least 15 minutes a day or more every day reading a variety of books and material. You'll be amazed at the impact this one small change can have on your life.

Seminars: Seminars can be great because they're an interpersonal, active way of learning. You're never too old to learn, and you can treat your life as if you were still in school (only now you get to choose the curriculum). But don't just choose any seminar; focus on finding ones that speak to your purpose and what resonates with what you're needing to learn.

Listening: Listen to uplifting, positive, affirmative and educational audios every single day. You can listen while running in the morning, doing laundry, or after work on your own free time while you relax. There's something very tangible about listening that connects with our thoughts, which is why I try to make this a daily habit.

If your idea of free time is to spend a few hours playing videogames or vegging out in front of the TV, you don't have to sacrifice every single weeknight to include these new habits. If you find places for them in your day where they don't feel like chores or burdens, you're more likely to follow through with them on a regular basis.

END OF CHAPTER ASSIGNMENT

In the assignment from the previous chapter, you generated a new thought that can help change your identity and attitude to something more productive. Now it's time to think about taking actions that align with your new affirmation.

For example, if you say "I am healthy," you could fix a healthy salad to eat every day to provide more nutrition in your diet. Or you might take up the habit of walking for 20 minutes every morning.

Your new action doesn't have to be a home run, but you should try to find something you can do every single day. Over time you can develop the strength to add more actions to your routine. But for now start with something that's uncomplicated and easy to incorporate into your daily schedule.

As your actions come into alignment with your thoughts you'll feel more powerful, which means you're taking control of your thoughts. However, don't be surprised if this starts a chain reaction of other positive thoughts throughout the day (and won't that be a bummer!).

CHAPTER FOUR

THE POWER OF EMOTION

Many people separate the idea of thoughts and feelings as if they're completely unique entities. But the reality is the way you feel *is* another form of thought. In other words, good and bad feelings are not only the result of thought, but are a part of thought itself.

Emotion plays a significant role in your thoughts, so much so that it can be hard to distinguish between the two. If someone insults you, you'll probably feel bad without thinking about it. But this doesn't mean you've stopped thinking, because your emotions are the result of your subconscious mind.

However, emotions aren't just results—they can also be catalysts for change. After all, what are emotions if not guiding feelings such as anxiety, fear, happiness, gratitude that are all meant to steer you in the right direction. They're your subconscious saying

"I'd like more of this, please!" or "No, this doesn't feel good so I'll avoid it."

You can't ignore the power of emotion if you want to change your thoughts for the better. Even your deepest, most superficial fantasies are imbedded with emotional content as they come from your subconscious.

Let's say you have the fantasy of one day owning a yacht. Are you fantasizing about the actual yacht? Or with how owning a yacht would make you feel? Chances are you don't picture yourself lazing around on deck, but piloting it with the wind in your hair and sailing off into the sunset. Ask someone why they want a motorcycle, and they'll most likely say they enjoy the freedom of being on the road with the wind whooshing around them and no cares in the world.

Deep down people don't want things—they want the feelings associated with things and experiences. As it turns out, feelings not only determine our goals and desires, but can be used to help us achieve them.

Emotions and Motivation

The word "emotion" is closely tied to the word "motivation" (they even have the same root: motion) because they both have the same goal of getting you in motion.

Most things in life have very basic sensations of pleasure and pain. Touch a hot pan and you'll feel the pain that tells you to let go. Drink a cold glass of water on a hot day, and you'll feel the pleasure associated with replenishing your body.

Our emotions are essentially there for the same reason: to help us as we interact with our environment. If you feel stuck at your job, or feel lonely and depressed, then you know there's a problem you need to address. Similarly, if you feel satisfied in your relationships, you know your actions have been healthy and appropriate.

If you've had problems with motivation, it's likely because your perception of emotions were lopsided. Think about going out for a run. If sitting on the couch and eating cheese doodles makes you feel good, you'll likely associate running with pain, laborious breathing, and denying yourself of your favorite snack. Having those sorts of negative emotional associations will block your motivation to get off the couch.

But what if you were to associate positive emotions with the actual experience of running? Maybe you like the feeling of getting out in nature, or how good you feel when you run, or how fabulous you look because your body is lean and healthy. When you focus on the positive aspects of exercise, you'll find the motivation to make it happen.

Of course running is going to feel a little uncomfortable as it is after all physical exercise. But what truly determines whether or not you will take action is how you perceive it in your mind. Remember: "As a man thinketh in his heart, so is he." Many of your habitual thoughts aren't tied up in their actual content, but are tied up because of the emotions you associate with them.

When you face a battle of willpower, it's often because you're fighting against your own emotions. It's a fight that's difficult to win because avoiding feeling unpleasant is an inherent instinct.

Cartoonist Scott Adams wrote in *Time* magazine that every time he goes to the gym he uses his cool-down time to enjoy a power shake and surf the Web on his smartphone. By giving himself rewards for his efforts, he creates a Pavlovian response where he associates going to the gym with both pain and pleasure. Needless to say he's found it easier to go to the gym.

Instead of fighting against using your emotions for motivation, you need to associate positive emotions with the actions you need to take. Adams' Pavlovian technique is a great example of cultivating a positive habit by attaching a reward, which eliminates the need to only focus on pain and misery and instead on the joy and benefits of the experience. For example, go hiking before you eat lunch. That way you work up an appetite while on the hike, but now the meal serves as a reward for your exercise.

If you use this principle with all your "unpleasant" habits, you'll be surprised at how the need for willpower begins to melt away, and motivation and action will become commonplace.

Using Emotions in Your Affirmations

Including positive emotions will supercharge your affirmations, and one of the most powerful emotions you can incorporate is gratitude. In fact, motivation expert Bob Proctor teaches that people should use affirmations that begin with "I am so happy and grateful now that..."

When you associate gratitude with your affirmations, you send your subconscious mind a signal that what you want already exists. You begin to behave and think like you've already accomplished your goals, which helps bring your reality into alignment with your desires.

Additionally, gratitude is a positive, healthy, feel-good emotion. When you feel gratitude you accept the universe for what it is and tell your subconscious "I'd like some more, please!"

Another aspect of using emotions in your affirmations to make them more powerful is the idea of having versus wanting. When you want something you're focusing on what you lack, and the emotions associated with your desire can be anything from loneliness to depression.

But when you have something you feel happiness, gratitude and a sense of peace, and you're excited because your life is already changed by the thing you have. When you use affirmations charged with positive emotions, you're sending yourself the message that what you want is already present in your life. These thoughts then are reflected in your actions, your beliefs, and ultimately your reality.

Upon hearing this people often say, "But how can I feel the emotions of having something if it's not actually there? I feel like I'm deluding myself because it's a total lie."

The response is to realize that every thought is part of the process of creating reality. By understanding this premise, you'll begin to see how just about everything you do—whether it's writing emails to your friends or talking to yourself in the mirror—is a positive affirmation.

When you unconsciously use negative affirmations like "I'm never going to find someone to love," you accept it unconditionally as your reality. You feel to the core of your being that you are lonely and unlovable, and something is wrong with you.

But why can't the reverse be true? Why can't you enjoy the act of creating things with your affirmations, thoughts and your actions? Why do we quickly accept negative thoughts as being valid, and positive thoughts as "delusional"?

When you begin to see how important it is to "have" instead of "want," you'll see this powerful process isn't about self-delusion but self-creation.

Thinking With Your Heart

James Allen's phrase isn't "As a man thinketh in his head..." He (or she) thinks in his (or her) heart, which can have different connotations. In many ways, the heart is the symbol of the subconscious mind, which isn't too concerned with logic and reason. It believes what it believes and feels what it feels, which is why emotions play such a powerful role in the development of your subconscious beliefs.

The attachments you create between a thought's content and its emotional meaning are what your subconscious takes to "heart." It doesn't matter if your belief seems outlandish or unattainable. If you regularly reinforce it with powerful emotions, you're eventually going to believe it.

If you have trouble seeing how this is possible, consider how easy it is to let negative thoughts become associated with negative feelings. When you're in a bad mood, it's easy to think with emotion. *Gosh, I'm so awkward,* you might think while beating yourself up with every word. Many people feel very comfortable wallowing in negative emotions, rather than leaving their comfort zone to experience something new and positive.

Thinking positive thoughts in conjunction with positive emotions isn't very different, as you're substituting one for the other with new thoughts and emotions. At first it may feel odd generating emotions along with your affirmations. You may think, *If*

I don't actually have that $100,000 job, how can I feel grateful or excited about it?

That's the wrong approach because it means you're looking for emotional resources rooted in logic. Emotions aren't logical as they're feelings, and believe it or not you can change them merely by altering your focus.

This may sound complicated, so let's break it down into simpler terms to show you how to take charge of your emotions:

> **Change Your Body Language:** If you're alone stand up, smile as big and goofy a smile as you can, and puff out your chest. Then say "I feel really happy!" Repeat the process, and expand your body language to imitate what you look like when you feel happy. What do you notice? You'll probably notice it's impossible not to feel happy once you align your body language with the emotion you want to feel. Even the simple act of smiling can alter your mood.

> **Stimulate Your Emotions Before an Affirmation:** Another way to control how you feel is to stimulate your emotions before trying an affirmation. If you want to feel happy, for example, search for online videos that show people smiling and laughing, or even dogs doing silly tricks if that's what makes you feel

good. When you feel yourself smiling, it's time for your affirmation.

Raw Determination: Napoleon Hill would tell people to command their subconscious mind to have new thoughts. Guess what? You can use raw determination to feel better by commanding yourself to feel a certain way. When combined with the other strategies listed in this book, you'll find that feeling better is not merely a benefit but inevitable.

This then is what it means to "think with your heart." Instead of reading your affirmations from a piece of paper without any emotions, you activate the areas of your brain you want to activate with emotions. In time your subconscious mind will tell you that if you're happy because of these thoughts, you should start changing the way you view X or Y. In turn, your life will change because your subconscious mind has taken notice of your new thoughts and feelings.

END OF CHAPTER ASSIGNMENT

During the exercise for the previous chapter you found a way to make your affirmation active. Now you're to find a way to attach positive emotions to that same affirmation, and you can start by using any (preferably all) of the three techniques you read in the previous section.

Please give ample consideration to the emotions you want to feel as they might differ depending on what kind of goals you have. For example, if your goal is to attract more wealth, you might want to focus on feelings of abundance, of relaxed living (who can feel stressed when they have a lot of money in the bank?), the environment you want to live in, and excitement for the future. If your goal is to attract more positive relationships, you can focus on feelings of confidence, poise, and the joy of helping others.

You need to remember to keep the affirmations and their associated emotions positive. Remember the "pink elephant" theory? You don't want to use negative thoughts like "I avoid bad decisions," because you're only focusing on bad decisions. Instead you should use a positive statement like "I make the right decisions."

So too should it be with your emotions. It's possible to associate bad emotions with what you don't want, but then you're focusing on the wrong thing and you'll get more of what you don't want. Does this make sense? By focusing your emotions on feeling good, you'll eventually start to feel good more and more until it becomes a habit. Considering your subconscious mind responds to habits, that's a very good prospect indeed.

THE POWER WITHIN YOURSELF

"People are anxious to improve their circumstances, but are unwilling to improve themselves. They therefore remain bound." This is a spectacular piece of wisdom from James Allen, because it gets us thinking not about the circumstances we have, but what kind of people we must be in order to produce those circumstances.

"The power of yourself" is all about realizing you're ultimately responsible for the life you create. If you want your outer world to improve, you're first going to have to improve your inner world (or self).

Let's say you struggle forming new relationships. If you feel unworthy or incomplete, how will that be reflected in your circumstances or personality? You'll turn people off because they'll sense you want something from them, and you don't feel whole or secure.

Who wants to hang out with someone who needs something from them?

On the other hand, if you're perfectly happy in your own company and feel good about yourself, there's a better chance you'll have good relationships as self-confidence is inherently attractive. Therefore, you shouldn't blame others for your loneliness or your lack of relationships, but what's going on inside your head and your heart.

It's pretty much the same for all circumstances in your life. Your outer abundance will reflect your inner abundance, and your outer lack will reflect your inner lack. If you want to change your circumstances, you must *become* the person in the circumstances you want to live in.

You can't separate the two, nor can you hope for magically improved circumstances by being the same person you are today. You must change if you want your circumstances to change, which isn't bad news. Instead, you should feel excited about having the power to change the world around you. It's an astounding fact that as you build inner strength, your outer world will also change.

You should feel very empowered instead of weakened by this knowledge. For example, if you want to build muscular strength, it's going to require you to become physically strong. You also need to keep your mental habits strong to keep you going to the gym even when you don't want to. It means struggling through your weakness, and eventually dismissing it as a reality.

Therein lies the power of the inner world that holds the key to just about everything you could possibly want. But it requires that you step up and take responsibility for your outer world.

So let's look deeper to find answers to changing your inner world for the better, and finally acknowledging the power you hold each and every day.

Be It Today – Don't Hope For It Tomorrow

Earlier I addressed the concept that says "there is no tomorrow." This is very important, not only because it's a bad idea to put off till tomorrow what you can do today, but because of the power today holds in changing your life.

Let's look at an example of freshman Dave who has enrolled at a new college. He had a few friends in high school, but his social skills and confidence let him down when he's presented with new challenges. So he goes to his classes not knowing anyone, and feels isolated and alone.

The most dangerous thought Dave can have is one day he'll be more confident. Why is this dangerous? Because if he keeps waiting for "one day" to come, it probably won't. If he hopes that tomorrow will be easier to be confident than it is today, he'll be severely disappointed.

Dave will fail to build self-confidence by procrastinating, returning to his habits, going back to his college dorm room to play videogames, and avoiding social interaction. He knows he wants to be confident, but keeps putting it off for a tomorrow that never comes.

Another way he could fail would be to focus on becoming a self-confident person. He could read a lot of blog posts and books about building charisma, making new friends, etc. But if he never applies what he learns, he'll become too focused on the act of *being* rather than the action of *becoming*.

This strategy won't work if you read everything about building muscle and losing fat without taking the time to change your diet and going to the gym more regularly. You won't make as much progress as someone who did all these things, even if they hadn't learned as much as you about becoming fitter and leaner.

This is why it's so important to think about change as occurring in the present. In the New Testament (which inspired a great deal of wisdom in *As a Man Thinketh*), we're told not to think about tomorrow because there's plenty to worry about today (which could be extended to the concept of change). As an individual you don't get to directly affect anything except the present moment.

In the case of Dave, the best strategy to become

confident and social wouldn't be to keep putting it off, or studying more about becoming more confident. Instead, it would be to take action today and not put it off till tomorrow, which is the main difference between *being* something versus *wanting* to be something.

Utilizing the strategy of "fake it till you make it," Dave talks more in classes, introduces himself to his dorm neighbors, and finds more social activities to join. As he bears witness to himself taking these actions, his self-perception will change. Even if his first social interactions don't go smoothly, he'll feel more social if he keeps at it. In fact, he'll stop "faking it" and will eventually have "made it," which is why *being* is so much more powerful than *wanting* to be.

When you make the decision to embody the changes you want, you can instantly change your self-perception. But if you keep wanting to be something else, your self-perception will never change.

You can't affect change to yesterday or tomorrow, but only for what's right in front of you today. You can remain on the sidelines of your life, preferring to watch other people succeed while you focus on how to succeed tomorrow. Or you can stand tall and proud and take action in the present moment.

This wisdom applies to more than self-confidence. If you want to be fit, then what can you do today? You can adapt the behavior of a fit person by going outside for a run and pushing yourself to make an extra lap, or preparing a healthy dinner.

Don't think about what you want to change; instead, decide what you want to have or be today. Life is too short, so there's no point in waiting.

Decide to Be Complete

Another concept many people struggle with is scarcity, or lacking pieces to their life's puzzle. Rather than feeling complete, they focus on what they don't have, which only serves to exacerbate the feelings of lack and want.

I spoke before about how powerful gratitude is. Part of the reason gratitude is such a valuable emotion is that it assumes a sense of wholeness (it's hard to be thankful for your life when you feel it's incomplete. Yet when you experience gratitude, how incomplete can you really feel?) People often experience gratitude when they feel an overabundance of blessings in their life. It's difficult to experience gratitude without focusing to some extent on how well our life is working out.

But what happens when this particular emotion is missing from your life? If you haven't felt truly grateful in a while, it might be because you view your life as incomplete. Instead of focusing on what you do have (abundance), you focus on what you don't have (lack).

If "as a man thinketh in his heart, so is he" is correct, you tend to get more of what you think about. If you feel incomplete as a human being, you're focusing on what you aren't or don't have versus what you truly are or do have.

You might say, "If I want a boat but don't have a boat, I can't be grateful for a boat I don't have!" which misses the point entirely. Remember, many fantasies aren't driven by the things we desire, but rather how we think we'll feel when we acquire those things. In the example of desiring a yacht, you can feel complete and in power even before you ever buy the yacht.

You can start changing lack into abundance by asking yourself a few key questions:

- What do I want that I don't have right now? (You might say "I want a corner office.")

- What feeling would I have by achieving that goal? ("A corner office will make me feel valued at work and successful in my career.")

- Can I experience those emotions right now if I truly decide to experience them? (Yes, you can!)

- What can I give the world around me in order to deserve my goal? ("I could put in more effort to make myself more valuable. I can feel relaxed and poised as if I already work in a corner office.")

By answering all these questions, you can construct an action plan that will make you feel as if you've already achieved your goal, which is exactly the kind of feeling you want to have. Because "as a man thinketh in his heart, so is he," you'll notice the world around you start to reflect this inner way of thinking.

You didn't change much about the world around you; all you did was to change the way you think and act. The achievement and gratitude you developed as a result of changing yourself will spill over into the world, which will in turn treat you differently and more positively. Feeling successful will cause others to treat you as though you're successful, which is one of the most important powers you hold within yourself. "As a man thinketh... so is he."

Become a Self-Fulfilling Prophecy

Have you ever noticed someone who didn't seem to have a lot of talent, connections, or discipline, yet seems to have that "special something"? They're usually someone who has a lot of desire for success, and have worked hard to prepare themselves for it. They believe success is inevitable, and their actions (the fruits of their thoughts) prove their intentions are spot on.

Maybe the dress code at their office is business casual, yet they dress just like all the managers do. Or they network with upper management, even though their current position doesn't require them to do so. Everything seems to work for them because they're living a life of "self-fulfilling prophecy." They believe so much in their own success that their behavior begins to shape their reality.

If you've ever heard career advice like "dress for the job you want, not the job you have," then you're familiar with this concept. This advice is another way of saying "rather than desire to change, simply decide to be."

Although a person who's living a life of self-fulfilling prophecy understands this intuitively, it can be frustrating from an outsider's perspective. Maybe you work very hard developing your skills to be as efficient and indispensable as possible. Yet you continually get passed over for promotions because you don't seem like management material.

Meanwhile, your colleague—the one living the self-fulfilling prophecy—doesn't put in the same work as you do, but is promoted into a higher position. Although management gives different reasons for his promotion, you know it's because he always "seemed" like management.

What you're seeing is a self-fulfilling prophecy at work, so the key is to making it work for you instead of against you. In classical literature the self-fulfilling prophecy was often used to relay tragedy. Someone who attempted to prevent a tragic prophecy ended up fulfilling it through their own fears.

Don't let the self-fulfilling prophecy work against you. Instead, make it work for you by deciding what to be and fulfilling that role in your thoughts and actions. Inhabit the role you desire, and people will begin seeing you in that role.

CHAPTER FIVE: THE POWER WITHIN YOURSELF

END OF CHAPTER ASSIGNMENT

In the previous chapter's assignment you were to associate emotions with your affirmation. In this chapter you were shown how to work on those emotions by completing the questions you read in the section "Decide to be Complete":

- What do I want that I don't have right now?

- What feeling would achieving that goal give me?

- Can I experience those emotions right now if I truly decided to experience them? If so, how?

- What can I give the world around me in order to deserve my goal?

These questions dig a little deeper by allowing you to find out why you truly want what you want. But now the focus should shift from the emotions you'll have, to it's time to go about life as if you already have those emotional needs met.

Why? Because you want the emotions you use to charge your affirmations to be the right ones. Your feelings are essentially "direct lines of communication" between your conscious and subconscious mind. It helps to use emotions if you want to send your subconscious mind a message. The better you understand your feelings, the more effective you'll be.

Use the positive emotions you've discovered during

this process such as gratitude, abundance, acceptance, etc. Then as you go about your daily routine, you'll do so positively since you know what you're working toward.

Have you ever met someone who felt the world owed them something? If you think the world should give you something, it means you know you don't have it and it focuses on lack. Therefore, the question "What can I give the world around me in order to deserve my goal?" is crucial, as it means you've stopped thinking about what you don't have versus what you believe you have. And following "as a man thinketh," you'll continue to suffer from lack as long as your thoughts run that way.

On the other hand, if you give the world something in order to deserve your goal, you're focusing on abundance and thinking about what you do have. After all, you can't give without the assumption that you already have, and you'll have more in your life as a result of giving.

CHAPTER SIX

MAKE YOUR CHANGE COMPLETE

The saying "one brick at a time" means even though you may have high aspirations, you can't control anything except for the one brick you have in your hand. So you might as well not dwell on the enormity of the work ahead of you and keep going.

But what if you lay only one brick at a time, and then give up because the stack doesn't seem to be getting any higher or wider? You stand back to see what you've accomplished, but realize a building without walls is about as good as no building at all.

If your thoughts have created your circumstances, you're going to have to undergo a massive change of attitudes and beliefs in order to implement change, but you have to tackle them one at a time.

Think about how many people last on a diet for even 90, 60, 30 or even 10 days. There are plenty of valid programs such as Atkins, South Beach, and Weight Watchers. Many people have had success with these diets, which affirms their strategies must have some validity. But if you've ever struggled with your weight, you know that attempting to change what you eat without any regard for the changes you need to make to your inner self will only result in failure.

If you've had a habit of eating poorly for many years, you've also had the thoughts and conditioning that allowed you to continue eating this way. Merely substituting bad food for healthier food isn't enough to ensure you'll stick to new habits. If you really want to change what you eat, your mind can't think about junk food or cheating. And once again, "as a man thinketh…" comes into play.

The success behind complete change is seeing your change through to the end by being sure your thoughts, beliefs, and attitudes all align with your new strategies. In this chapter, you'll find out some ways you can do exactly that.

Eliminate Negative Influences

The first thing you need to do to make sure your change is complete is to do a bit of "house-cleaning." You probably accumulated many conflicting thoughts and habits over the years that keep reinforcing the way you live. If you really do want to change, you're going to have to completely eliminate these negative thoughts and habits. So let's look at a few ways to begin the process.

Eliminate external "stimuli": Let's return to the example of sticking to a new diet. You've decided to start today, but haven't gone to the grocery store to stock up on the food you'll need. Your kitchen is probably filled with stuff you're not supposed to eat. Rather than let them taunt and tempt you to cheat, you can toss them in the garbage and head to the store. Eliminating the temptations will give you a much better chance at avoiding cheating (the same goes for the bag of chips in your desk drawer at work, the bag of cookies in your gym bag, or the candy bars in your car's glove compartment).

Nip your bad habits in the bud: If you've had a series of bad habits that have contributed to your circumstances, you know how powerful they can be. In fact, you should eliminate them as soon as possible so they don't have time to grab hold of your thoughts. Maybe you have the habit of watching an hour of television right after work. You come home, plop down in your favorite chair, and reach for the remote control. Nip that habit in the bud by hiding the remote and taping a note to the TV that says "Go for a walk!"

Change your environment: Because habits can be highly social, you may need to change your environment in order to effect change. This is when the adage "you're the average of your five closest friends" comes into play. Being around negative influences can weaken your resolve. Your hunger to feel social acceptance may sacrifice your deeper desires, but please don't let this happen. Instead, try to find ways to be involved with positive/motivated people and healthier social situations, even if it means volunteering at charities simply to get out of the house!

Eliminate yourself from the equation as much as possible: You're ultimately responsible for your good or bad choices, which means you'll sometimes have to do your own intervention. If you're trying to quit smoking, go to the places where you buy cigarettes and give them a letter with your picture that says they're not to sell to you. If you find this too difficult because you're worried you'll never smoke again, you were never really invested in quitting. Find ways to eliminate yourself from your habits, and stick to them!

Of course, simply eliminating bad influences isn't enough to create a complete change in your life as there are more levels beyond laying one brick at a time.

Make it Easy on Yourself

Once you've eliminated bad stimuli and external influences, you should start thinking about the positive ways you can make a complete change. A good attitude to develop is, "I'm my own personal assistant." So think of all the ways a personal assistant might help you eliminate bad habits, and start doing those things for yourself.

Let's say you want to stick to a diet, but when you go to the office you never bring a bagged lunch. So you end up buying expensive calorie-laden lunches that knock you out of your efforts to eat healthier.

The key is to make the better choice the easier choice as well. As human beings we have a tendency to avoid pain and seek pleasure. So the key is not to indulge these instincts, but to use them to our advantage.

For example, one reason people struggle with eating fast food is it's more convenient to go to a drive-through than it is to go home and prepare a healthy meal. You don't even have to get out of your car to make poor eating decisions. Just look at the board, tell them what you want, hand them the money and voila! Your food is immediately accessible.

If you're going to change bad eating habits, you need to make healthier choices more convenient. So for starters, jot down the times of day when you notice yourself reaching for or purchasing poor food options, and think about what you can do to make healthier choices more convenient during those times.

Let's say you hate making breakfast in the morning, so you always go to the drive-through on the way to work. Instead, you could take an hour every Sunday evening and cook five healthy breakfasts, put them in the refrigerator or freezer, and microwave them every morning. Which is more convenient? Thirty seconds standing at a microwave? Or taking time to go to the drive-through?

Another obvious option is to pack your own lunches, but you don't have to stop there. If you keep buying soda in cans because they're easy to grab and open, why not replace them with water bottles? Buying water bottles in bulk is not only convenient, but healthier and costs a lot less.

There's always a solution when you give it some thought, so don't be afraid to get a little creative. Remember, a good solution won't always present itself immediately, so take your time to find ways that work for you.

Make Your Goal a Central Driving Purpose in Your Life

James Allen wrote that once you know your purpose, you shouldn't look right or left during the journey, but look for the straight path that leads to its achievement. (Napoleon Hill called it a "chief, definite purpose" that guides all your actions and thoughts.) Plus, you need to exclude your doubts and fears as if they were never part of the journey.

However you view it, the point is that focus is the key to success. If you want to completely change your life, then making your goal a chief definite purpose is of utmost importance. Why? Because your focus—your attention—is one of the most powerful tools you have at your disposal. But if you don't focus it laser-tight on your goal, you're misusing it and all your efforts will go to waste.

A good analogy is a magnifying glass. Held too far away from an object, it makes things look hazy. Your answers and choices will appear hazy when your focus is too general and unspecified. But when you hold the magnifying glass closer, the image becomes clearer. Therefore, the smaller and more specific your focus, the clearer your decisions and choices.

It's easy to cast doubts aside when you know what you want, because doubts linger when you're not sure if you're following the right path. When you know deep within your heart your path is the right one, and that your dreams mean more to you than people can understand, you won't worry about whether or not you're making the right choices.

This is very important to understand, because even the straightest path between you and your goals can be fraught with obstacles. It may require you to take leaps of faith, climb the highest mountains, or cross bridges you never thought you could cross.

So the point here is if you don't have a definite goal guiding your actions, when would you have the courage to overcome obstacles or the motivation to even try? People who don't know what they want in life will arrive at an obstacle, observe how hard it is, and think, *You know what? I'm not so sure I want this goal enough to take this risk.*

James Allen said, "He that seeketh findeth." But this doesn't refer to a casual seeking of your goals; otherwise, everyone would stumble onto theirs all the time and that's not how the world works. But if you focus your efforts on a single goal and don't stop until you reach it, you're beginning to understand the meaning of "he that seeketh findeth."

And speaking of focus...

The Power of Prolonged Focus

You don't truly begin to experience the raw power of thought until you develop the power of prolonged focus.

Focus is a major challenge as we have a million things running through our head all day. We want to accomplish X while thinking about Y. We want to finish A, but can't stop thinking about B and C. We have all sorts of errands to run, projects to finish, and by the time we go to bed we look back on our day and wonder what we really accomplished.

However, prolonged focus is different. Have you ever had a day where you worked on just one thing for several hours? How did you feel afterwards? Chances are, you felt changed. You felt as if the work became easier after a period of time, and that you didn't even have to struggle to think about it. Your prolonged focus was enough to shift your reality so that outside noise or distractions didn't bother you.

Think about it this way: Many people struggle to get to sleep, only to wake up in the morning and feel like nothing could possibly be as comfortable as their bed. So why was it so difficult to go to sleep, then just as difficult to wake up? Many people call it "sleep inertia," which is the momentum that's occurred from many hours of rest. Like a train it takes a while to get going. But once it gets its momentum and speed on the tracks, it will take a while for it to slow down.

This then is the power of prolonged focus. If you can focus on single goals for several hours during the day and for strings of days at a time, you'll notice your reality changes as a side effect of the momentum you're building, which would make it harder not to think about your goals and the new subjects of your focus. And since "as a man thinketh in his heart, so is he," you begin to realize the vast implications of this kind of specific focus.

Everything in life has its own specific momentum. If the earth stopped spinning, we'd all fly off into space. So it's impossible to avoid momentum unless you always stand still and accomplish nothing, which is why it can be difficult to quickly change your thoughts and habits.

Like a train, it can take a while before you can get your new thoughts and habits up to full speed. But if you stick with it and continue focusing on pushing the train forward, eventually its momentum will carry you forward and soon you'll have a hard time stopping!

END OF CHAPTER ASSIGNMENT

In the assignment for Chapter Three, you were to find an action to correspond with your affirmations. This time, you're going to look for new habits to correspond with your affirmations.

Look at the environment around you, and ask yourself how it can be changed to one that fosters your goals. If the music you listen to is too depressing to foster happiness, stop listening to it. If the evening news you watch gets you upset, don't watch it. If the lighting in your office makes it hard to read or see your computer monitor, install proper lighting to make things easier for you. Write down every detail, and then start fixing things to make your environment conducive for your goals.

Additionally, make sure you follow through with the advice in this chapter by eliminating negative influences and replacing them with positive ones that help make your new goals easier to accomplish.

Let's say you want to be a literary writer, but you spend a lot of your time reading the news. What if you shifted to reading fiction in some of the world's best literary magazines? Chances are you'd gain much more insight into what it takes to be a good writer, and you wouldn't miss the news one bit.

Small changes like this can add up, so make sure you closely examine your habits to see where you can make positive changes.

CHAPTER SEVEN

PLEASURE VERSUS PAIN

The previous chapter discussed avoiding pain and moving toward pleasure. Touching a hot pan will be painful, and drinking cold water on a hot day gives pleasure and relief. But when the balance between pleasure and pain gets out of whack, it can lead to some pretty bad long-term consequences.

Sometimes vices are associated with pleasure when they should be associated with pain. A smoker with a two-pack a day habit knows smoking causes all sorts of pain. Maybe their spouse hates their habit, or they're sick of their clothes smelling badly, or they're worried about the long-term health effects such as cancer. Yet the smoker associates their habit with pleasure, relaxation and stress release, even though they know smoking can cause negative consequences to their life.

So what gives? Skewed perceptions and manipulation of the subconscious are to blame. We have become a society of instant gratification where short-term pain and pleasure is more acceptable than long-term joy and satisfaction.

Reversing bad fortune and reaping abundant rewards will require you to reverse the "polarity" of pleasure and pain. And not surprisingly it all begins with the way you think.

Adding Information to Your Choices

Being human means we have free will and are capable of making decisions on our own. But how often do you feel well-equipped to make the right choices? In many cases we make bad decisions when we're in a jam, often because we don't know any better.

Sometimes when we're about to make a bad choice, it's because we don't have enough information to make the right choice. For example, we know we're supposed to wear a seatbelt when we get in a car. To change the bad habit of not wearing your seatbelt into a good habit of wearing it, you could research statistics to find out how many people die in car crashes versus those who live because they were wearing a seatbelt. Or you might read testimonials online from people who say that wearing a seatbelt saved their life. Eventually, you'd make the decision to wear a seatbelt because the good outweighed the bad.

Adding information to your choices will change your perception of pleasure and pain. Where you previously thought wearing a seatbelt was constrictive and annoying, you now equate wearing one as providing safety and security. Eventually you'll be conditioned to never driving without wearing one.

Although pain is pain and pleasure is pleasure, these experiences are subjective to the individual. Smokers believe cigarettes are pleasurable after eating, while others can't stand the smell of smoke.

So what's the difference? It's not the smoke itself, because otherwise everyone would enjoy it. It's the way people think about or react to the smoke that defines the pleasure and pain received from it.

Information is an invaluable weapon in your arsenal for change. Consider how someone who hates cigarette smoke will smell it and instantly think about lung cancer, emphysema, allergies to smoke, etc. They associate smoking with a whole host of negative connotations because they prefer to focus on that information.

Of course, there's more to the story as many cigarette smokers continue to smoke even though they know the dangers. "I know how bad it is for me," they'll say, "but I can't stop." At that point, you need to dig even deeper to find ways to change your perceptions of pain and pleasure.

Ending the Cycle of Rationalization

The power of rationalization – one of the most powerful tools in our "thought arsenal"—usually works against us instead of on our behalf. Rationalization doesn't empower us, but rather is a tool to help us feel better about making inferior decisions. It can completely manipulate a conscious positive decision into an unconscious destructive one.

How many times have you tried to stop a bad habit by telling yourself *this is the last time*, or *I'll start changing on Monday*? These are examples of rationalizing current behavior by mortgaging something else in our realities (in this case the future).

Rationalizations come in all shapes and sizes. *I shouldn't go out for a run today because it's cold and I don't have a scarf. So all I need is a scarf to make sure I run every day!*

Ending an illogical cycle of rationalization starts with identifying the ones that are hurting you. So let's look at some different types:

> **Procrastination:** This is one of the most dangerous types of rationalization as it makes you believe you haven't given up your dreams, when in reality you're putting them off (and possibly indefinitely). By saying "I'll accomplish X and Y, but not until after ____ ___happens," you're giving up today's oppor-

tunities and experiences for tomorrow where they may or may not happen. Therefore, the lie is there is no tomorrow.

"I'm just missing this one thing": Making a poor decision because you don't think you're quite ready may be a simple rationalization. For example, you might think, *I'll be ready to give up smoking once I buy that vapor cigarette*. But you never buy it, and the cycle continues. Start today with what you have today.

"One day I'll be strong enough to do this, but not today": Strength doesn't come from waiting – it comes from resistance and challenge. If you can't find the courage to take action today, it will be harder to find the courage to take action tomorrow because you'll be stuck in negative momentum.

Breaking the cycle of rationalization depends on what your particular problem is and what you need to focus on. Rationalization holds one and only one power over you: it grants your emotional and physical needs without having confronted the actual issue. Therefore, in order for you to stop rationalizing, you have to take away its power.

When you tell yourself *I'll finish this tomorrow* or *I can do this at the end of the week*, you feel as though you're taking action even though you aren't.

Through rationalization, you grant yourself an emotional victory without the actual victory. The way to end the cycle of rationalization is to prevent this from happening by changing your perception of the rationalization itself.

For example, think about how much harder it will be to complete a project at the end of the week if you haven't started. But if you start working on it today and half of it's done by the end of the week, think how easy it will be to finish the other half because you've gained momentum.

Getting Over the Need to Sacrifice

I was raised with the notion that "no pain" means "no gain." When I played basketball the practices were tough and rigorous, and I was tired and miserable. Sure, there were positive results associated with this activity, because I was playing sports, getting exercise, and having fun at the same time.

But I eventually grew up, graduated from college, and joined the real world where I was responsible for my own body because there were no more basketball practices to go to. And since I had the mentality of "no pain, no gain," guess what happened? Because I had learned to associate improving my body with hard work and sacrifice, I thought going to the gym or running meant I'd have to experience pain. I had becomes so conditioned to feel only pain with exercise that I ceased to feel the pleasure associated with getting healthier. So I quit taking care of my body.

The moment I realized I had to change my mental conditioning started when I finally quit my three pack-a-day cigarette smoking habit. I had tried to quit many times over the years, but all I thought about was what I was sacrificing by not smoking. It felt like I was being denied one of life's greatest pleasures, and was getting nothing in return. With that kind of attitude, is it any wonder why I failed to quit? It was logical that I'd start again if I thought quitting smoking was depriving myself of all that pleasure!

"There's nothing like a cigarette after you drink a cup of coffee, or when you're drinking," smokers often say. They talk about having cigarettes in a very positive light, so it's no surprise they struggle to give it up. They're rationalizing their addiction so they can experience the pleasure they've come to associate with smoking.

When I was trying to quit smoking I only focused on what I was giving up. It felt like a sacrifice, a denial of the great feelings smoking gave me after a meal or with a cup of coffee. I finally realized that as long as I thought this way, I wouldn't be able to quit.

So I took a different approach and began to associate non-smoking with being able to take a deep breath. I visualized being able to wake up in the morning and not cough throughout the day with a hacking cough (which was horrible, as it felt like I was going to hack up my lungs). When I shifted my focus from what I would be sacrificing to what would be gained by not smoking, the results became immediately evident.

You will have to learn this lesson if you hope to effect lasting change in your life. If you view going to the gym as a thankless chore, then it's going to be just that. But if you make the decision to go to the gym because it will make you feel good and that it's healthy for you, then you're getting somewhere.

Associating Pain with Bad Habits

We indulge in bad habits because they're comfortable, and to some degree give us pleasure (or at the very least momentarily deny ourselves pain). We have to stop associating pleasure with our bad habits, and start associating pain with them in order to quit. (You'll receive some tips for how to do that in the upcoming end of chapter assignment.)

But let's first address some key concepts for associating pain with activities you want to avoid. How will you ever get over a bad habit if you continue to view it as something that gives you pleasure? If you think of it as something that brings you joy, then giving it up will require some form of sacrifice and yes, it's going to feel painful.

Here are some tips for associating bad habits with pain and not with pleasure:

Concentrate on the consequences of the action—not the action itself: For example, if you want to quit smoking, you can reverse your thoughts about pain and pleasure by focusing on the consequences of the action (the potential for lung cancer, the constant coughing, the chemical dependence, etc.) When you realize that no action can be separated from its consequences, you'll see just how painful the habit really is.

Find the pleasure in giving up the bad habit: I found pleasure in the fact that I could wake up every day without a coughing attack. So for me, making the decision to quit was easy because I got more pleasure out of being able to breathe and not cough than the consequences (the pain) associated with smoking. I've never looked back because my brain was finally in congruence with the decision I wanted to make.

Continually remind yourself about pain and pleasure: It's important to reinforce these changes on a regular basis. If you're trying to lose weight, keep reminding yourself how good it feels to no longer feel bloated and sluggish from all that junk food you've been eating. Think about how good it feels to check on your progress in the mirror rather than fearing how you'll look when you go into public. Keep reminding yourself what's pleasurable about your new choices and what's painful about your old choices, and the results are sure to follow.

It's difficult to overcome our embedded concepts of pain and pleasure. No matter how much willpower we think we have, we can't avoid it. But the good news is we do have the power to change our perceptions of pleasure and pain, which will guide us to the decisions we want to make in the future. And that's why our thoughts are so powerful.

END OF CHAPTER ASSIGNMENT

You'll need a 3x5 notecard for this exercise. First, think of a habit that has been causing you problems and write it on the top of the card. For instance, you might list "biting my nails" or "smoking two packs of cigarettes a day" or "not exercising."

Next, list all the problems that are a direct or indirect result of that bad habit. For example, if your habit is biting your nails, you might write "my nails are never long enough to scratch with." Or "I'm self-conscious when people look at my hands." Any negative consequences as a result of your bad habit – no matter how small or odd it seems—should be listed.

Then flip the card over and write down each problem in a different way. Now say "I detest biting my nails because…" and then list one of the problems you originally wrote. The key to this exercise is you're focusing on the pain caused by your bad habits, and are no longer lying to yourself because these painful consequences really do exist.

You're changing your focus to alter your perception, so you also need to list any past painful memories associated with the habit. For instance, if your smoking has negatively affected others, write it down which will keep you honest when you say "I detest smoking because…"

Now carry this card around with you everywhere you go. Put it in your wallet, purse or briefcase and take it to work with you, to the grocery store, to the gym. You could even put it in a holder on your keychain to make it easier to remember. Then every time you feel tempted to indulge in your bad habit, take out the card and remind yourself why your habit isn't so pleasurable.

This isn't an exercise in self-rationalization, but rather a way to break free of self-delusion. In the past you probably justified your bad habits by rationalizing you could quit soon, or it was the last time you were going to do it. But all those rationalizations accomplished was to keep you feeling just enough emotional pleasure to continue with the pain caused by your habits.

"Rationalize" phonetically sounds like "rational lies." So stop the rationalization (the lies), start focusing on the pain your bad habits have caused you, and the truth will set you free!

CHAPTER EIGHT

BELIEVING IS SEEING

The phrase "seeing is believing" is a bunch of hogwash! I can't tell you how many people have come to me with questions that come from deep-seated assumptions they didn't even know they had. Some people feel predestined to have a certain medical condition because of their family history, so they literally "see it before it's there."

For human beings, believing is seeing. We aren't creatures who can digest every single piece of information surrounding us—we are creatures of focus. When we drive, we focus on what's happening on the road and ignore what might be happening elsewhere.

For the most part, this serves us well. But when our beliefs become negative, it shifts our perceptions to only detect the negative in our surroundings and you can guess the consequences of that.

Have you ever bought a new car only to notice the same one everywhere you go? It's not that the car magically appeared; it's that your perceptions changed. Your focus shifted what you're capable of detecting from the glut of information around you.

It's the same with our beliefs and what we see on a daily basis, which is why it's important to realize that humans don't work on a "seeing is believing" basis. To the contrary: We work on a "believing is seeing" basis, and the implications this simple concept has for your life can be astounding.

Accepting Responsibility for Your Circumstances

Accepting responsibility for your circumstances is one of the most powerful things you can do, because it means you own your power. Sure, you might not like what you've created for yourself thus far. But the reality is if you had the power to create it, you also have the power to change it.

Another important aspect of accepting responsibility is to begin questioning your beliefs. Your beliefs don't exist in a vacuum—they interact with the world. They mold your perceptions, they change how others perceive you, and they ebb and flow over time. That's why accepting responsibility for your circumstances means you must also accept responsibility for the beliefs that have shaped your world.

Your question at this point should be "Apparently I've created the circumstances I'm faced with. So what deeply-held beliefs do I have that got me here?" For example, let's say you aren't in a relationship even though you'd really like to find a life mate. What kind of beliefs might affect your ability to attract that special someone? Beliefs like "I'm not handsome," or "I'm not attractive enough to get their attention" can certainly be culprits.

Think about the effects these beliefs can have on your life. If you believe "I'm not handsome," what must you also believe? You might start thinking your self-worth isn't as valuable as the worth of others who are more attractive than you. You might think that if you're not handsome, then there's little point in grooming, buying nice clothes, etc., because other people will see through the façade. Your belief that you're not handsome ends up making you less handsome, which is why **believing is seeing**.

If you want to change your reality, you're going to have to start with your beliefs. When you look at your circumstances and accept responsibility for what you've created, you begin to question those beliefs, and that's the first critical step to changing them.

Don't know where to start? Below are some really good ideas to get you dislodged and on your way!

Choosing New Beliefs

I like to remind people that their minds are equipped to make choices. But they tend to leave their choices up to the habits and routines that comprise their day-to-day living, instead of using the part of the brain that can choose wisely.

Here's a notion to consider: What if you could choose your beliefs (maybe you think you already do)? By now you should be familiar with the concept of "you reap what you sow." Beliefs also apply to this principle, because we reap them based on what we've sowed.

Many people think their beliefs will always be their beliefs, and they're ironclad and unchangeable. Have you ever spoken to someone with low self-esteem, tried to cheer them up, or inspire them about their future prospects? It can be difficult to impossible to get through to them. Because if they're so dead-set in their beliefs that they don't budge, it's like they literally have a wall up in front of them.

But beliefs aren't as ironclad as you might think. Can you think of some things you believed five years ago that you no longer believe today? "Gosh," you might say. "I'm barely the same person I was five years ago." What about what you believed as a child versus what you now believe as an adult?

"Believe" it or not, your beliefs are very malleable. Just because they're difficult to change overnight doesn't mean they can't be changed (and sooner than you think!).

Choosing a new belief first requires making a conscious decision. If your subconscious mind is the boat, your conscious mind is the rudder steering it where to go. Sure the boat ebbs and flows with the water around you (your circumstances), but ultimately you're the one who chooses who gets in the boat with you and where it's going to sail off to.

You can shift the rudder of your life by taking action toward a new belief. For example, if your belief changes from "I'm an okay parent" to "I'm a great parent!" you could take action that reflects the new belief such as watching your kids more closely, being more attentive, doing homework with them, and taking time to make a difference in their lives.

Remember, thought and action working together does more to shift your reality than through thought or action alone. At first it might seem difficult to adopt a new belief. After all, you figure your beliefs are based on evidence and reality. So how can you shift them when you know you're attempting to "manipulate" yourself into believing something new?

But beliefs aren't reality; rather, they shift the reality of your focus. Think on this for a moment as it's very important you understand this concept.

Beliefs shift reality of your focus.

Would you look through an unfocused camera lens and say "That looks fuzzy, but it'll do." Or would you focus the lens, shifting its perspective until it presents the reality with which you're most pleased? "Oh, that looks nice and clear. That's how it's supposed to look!"

Choosing a new belief is like shifting the focus in a lens. The reality around you doesn't change—at least not right away—but your perspective will. And when you consider the enormity of the world, you begin to realize there may have been things you dismissed before that didn't enter your perspective. But it was only through a shift in belief that you started to detect them.

Creating New Circumstances

One of the reasons "believing is seeing" is that sometimes you don't see an accomplishment with your eyes until your mind has seen it first. Believing it in your subconscious mind makes the connection to your conscious mind, which causes your eyes to sit up and take notice.

In this context, seeing what you want to exist before it exists in reality is called "vision." Powerful leaders are described as "visionaries" because they see reality before it unfolds. But there is nothing prophetic about the ability to see something before it exists, because it's an act of creation of which every mind is capable.

Did you ever have a toy as a child or a project as an adult that required assembly? You didn't know how it would look when it was finished because you hadn't assembled it yet, so you referred to the instructions to see how it would look. That finished version didn't actually exist, but since your mind became committed to the vision, eventually through action and thought you made it a reality.

It's the same thing with jigsaw puzzles. You can start with an entire box of mismatched pieces with only the picture on the box top to guide you. You set about putting the pieces together, trusting that with enough dedication you'll eventually have the whole thing completed and the reality will match your vision.

So why don't we do that in other areas of our lives? Why do we save our vision for games and hobbies when we can apply it every single day to things that can fundamentally change our life?

Creating new circumstances requires creating a vision for yourself and committing to that vision. Just as you might refer to the box top as you work on a jigsaw puzzle, so should you create a vision of the reality you want to create.

The more specific, the better. When you think of your vision as a jigsaw puzzle, you realize that all your questions will be answered when the puzzle is finished. The image you see on the box top is complete, which is why your vision (your goals) should be as specific and complete as possible. It should be your "guiding box" that allows you to look at today's actions and wonder whether or not they've been the right ones. Your goals should be the "guiding star" that tells you whether or not you need to adjust course by shifting your rudder.

Ask the Right Questions

Creating new circumstances isn't always easy, but the process itself is simple. Once you create and commit to a new vision, you know what you have to do because you can ask yourself the right questions. You can use this principle no matter how small or large your dreams are.

For example, let's say you've been alone all your life and your goal is to build a budding, active social life full of loving people. As an introvert you've never been able to approach someone you know, much less a stranger. But your goals are ambitious because you're tired of being disconnected from people.

Should you be worried about whether or not you've set your goals too high? Of course not! You should use this opportunity to discover the answers to practical questions. Approach the problem as if you just emptied the puzzle pieces onto a table, and need to look at the picture on the box top to start putting them together.

Instead of saying "I want to make new friends, but I'm too shy to even make eye contact," you should reframe it as a question: "What can I learn that will make it easier to make more eye contact with people?"

When you reframe your challenge as a question, you make it a problem to be solved rather than one that rules your life. You can continue asking yourself more questions until you realize you're making your vision come true, no matter how lofty your goals and no matter where you started from.

Refuse to Indulge Negative Beliefs

If you've ever gone to a petting zoo, you know they sometimes let you feed the animals. Then you come upon a dangerous animal such as a bear or lion and see a sign that says "Do Not Feed the Animals!" You need to take a similar approach to your negative beliefs. Rather than indulging them and wallowing in self-pity, simply refuse to continue feeding them (otherwise, they can bite your head off!).

"Feeding" a belief means attention is the food of thought. If you pay attention to something, you're feeding your beliefs accordingly. Have you ever noticed that when you hold a deep-seated belief, you tend to brush aside evidence to the contrary? Your belief holds on to its position because you're unwilling to pay attention to the other side of the mirror. Similarly, have you ever noticed that people change their beliefs simply because they've changed their environment and what they pay attention to?

No matter what, you're always feeding beliefs. At this very moment you're feeding your beliefs by reading this book, and you're helping yourself because you're paying attention to positive messages.

But not all messages are positive, which is why it's important not to indulge in them in order to feed your negative beliefs. And your refusal to indulge your negative beliefs starts at the conscious level. Just as you choose not to buy into them, you must choose different things to pay attention to which isn't as hard as it sounds.

Consider all the things you pay attention to:

- Fiction and non-fiction books

- Music

- Television shows

- Movies

- Audiotapes

- Motivational speeches

- Social media

- Internet message boards and forums

- Emails

- Text messages

- Conversations

- Radio talk shows

- Political rhetoric

The list goes on and on. If you don't take charge of your attention, then your beliefs will be left to the whims of whatever stimuli you choose to indulge. If you want to reap better rewards, you're going to have to start sowing in different places and place your attention on different (more positive) things.

No matter how small the effects may seem, everything you pay attention to affects your life in one way or another. Then is when you realize you have the power to no longer harbor beliefs that will never properly serve you.

END OF CHAPTER ASSIGNMENT

Remember, your beliefs are the lens through which you view the world. For this chapter's assignment, you should start to examine the beliefs you carry around with you every day.

Get out a piece of paper and write down at least ten beliefs that don't serve you. For each one write two or three ways in which they have a negative impact. For example, believing "I'm not wealthy" can create laziness because you believe there are no rewards to work hard for.

Now take each of those beliefs and turn them on their head by writing the positive impacts they have on your life. But rather than focus on the actions you can take this very moment, drill down for evidence that the belief may be true.

For example, if your belief is "I am wealthy," write down a few reasons why it's true. It may be difficult to think of things, because searching through a lifetime of thoughts can be hard. But as you dwell on the belief, you'll realize there is a great deal of wealth in your life.

First, you have a pen and paper (or a laptop) to write with when others don't. You likely have a warm place to sleep and a roof over your head, which is a luxury to many people. Even though you have bills to pay you have money in the bank, cash in your wallet, and you can buy many things at a moment's notice.

The key is to realize your beliefs shape your reality by shaping what your mind sees. Tackle this same exercise for all ten of the negative beliefs you listed, and you'll begin to see just how warped your reality may have been all along.

CHAPTER NINE

DREAM BIG

Think about the best dreams you've had while sleeping. Maybe you've dreamt about flying. You felt the wind in your hair, your arms were spread wide like a bird, you saw land far below you, and nothing was in front of you but open sky. Of course it's a silly dream because you can't actually fly like a bird, but it seemed very real at the time. You wake up and it can take a while to become grounded back in reality.

In our waking life, our boldest dreams are the ones that matter most. Sadly many people have forgotten how to dream. They make compromises to their life, and forget they were children once and that it felt good to dream big.

If you reap what you sow, why plant only grass or a small garden? When people create victory gardens they want the brightest flowers, the tallest bushes and the greenest grass. Why do we seem to forget the same ambition when it comes to the tending of our lives?

There's a powerful quote that many people attribute to Benjamin Franklin: "Most men die at twenty-five, and aren't buried until they are seventy-five." Of course, he's talking about the death of dreams. If you want to utilize the full power of your thoughts and your actions, you're going to have to remember what it was like to dream big then do it!

The Power of Lofty Dreams

At some point in their life, many people abandon big dreams and sacrifice their goals for easier, more attainable (and often unfulfilling) ones. Or they keep putting off their dreams for "someday" (and as we've discussed, someday probably never comes).

James Allen wrote "Dream lofty dreams. And as you dream so shall you become." If it's true that as we dream so we become, then the importance of dreaming big can't be understated. Our time on earth is special and extremely short, and we're selling ourselves short if we don't try to go after big ambitions.

The power of big dreams is that they inspire us to take risks. And in taking those risks, we prove we're ready to pay the price because the rewards during the journey are worth it. We become better people when we pursue better dreams, because they require a great deal of concentrated effort and patience to achieve.

Imagine a young man walking into a bar with

his friends. They're all single, so they're naturally looking for young women to talk to. He sees a woman more beautiful than anyone he's ever seen before. But his friends press him to throw darts, or to talk to two friendly but uninteresting women at a table across the bar.

He can't keep his eyes off her, and everyone begins to disappear except him and the woman. The young man knows approaching her comes with great risk. He can feel it in his gut as the very thought of talking to her fills it with butterflies. He weighs playing darts with his friends (which is safe), or possibly meeting the love of his life, which is a big dream considering he never met her before. He finally summons the courage to talk to her, walks over to her and... does it really matter what happens next? That's your vision and your reality, so make it what you will.

He's grown as a man through the sheer act of summoning the courage to give meeting the woman a chance. He's taken an action that whispered to him, *You're worthy of great things in your life*. Even though his friends tease him and a cold beer is waiting for him – and playing darts would have been the safe thing to do—he knows intuitively that big dreams are the ones that make life worth living.

If it's true that you become what you think about, then of course you should dream big. If it's true that you have control of the rudder, why wouldn't you steer the ship to the best places on the map? Wouldn't you brave the harshest storms and driest droughts if you knew that what waited for you at the end of your journey were your dreams?

That's how it should be in life. We're not here to be mediocre versions of ourselves, but to live fully. If that includes working hard, then we should aim to make our work a labor of love. Doing it any other way is a dishonor to our dreams.

Dreams are magnetic, and big dreams even more so as they motivate us to push past failure, ignore our doubts, and to harbor nothing but faith that our journey will be complete. Dream big and big actions will follow!

The Difference Between Fantasies and Goals

Well, that's all well and good, you may be thinking. *But I've had big dreams since I can remember, and none of them have been achieved. What gives?* Without knowing it, you may be thinking about the distinction between fantasies and goals. On the surface there's not much difference, so you think about them equally as often.

You might daydream about your fantasies coming into alignment with reality. *If you become what you think about, why am I not a playboy astronaut basketball star millionaire? Because that's what I fantasize about!*

The difference between a fantasy and a goal is that

a fantasy is a wish and a goal can become a reality. Rather than goal-affirming "this is how my reality is [or can be]," the fantasy's affirmation is "I wish this was my reality." It's a subtle distinction, but it can make a powerful difference in your life.

If you continue to wish something new into your life, you'll always be focused on its lack of presence. "Wishing your life away" means continually putting off your big dreams into the future, when really you want to experience the reality in the here and now.

Imagine if you were to look in the mirror and "wish" your way to success. You take the time to muster all the faith and emotion you have. But then you say something non-affirmative like "One day I hope to be a basketball star" which is a bit better than "I'm not good at basketball," but it doesn't hit the core feeling of *being* a basketball star. It's a place to start, but eventually you're going to want to feel your dreams playing out in the present.

Most people don't take the time to invest this much effort into their fantasies. They relegate them to dark corners in their subconscious, and never give them the attention and emotion a real goal requires.

If you say "Supposedly, I become what I think, but I think about my fantasies all the time and none of them happen," you may not realize the subtle ways in which you're shooting your fantasies in the foot. After you're done daydreaming you come back to reality and think, *Ho-hum, back to my real boring life*, and it's become a self-fulfilling prophecy.

You need to be careful, because the kinds of messages you send to your subconscious can negate all the positive, affirmative thought work you just accomplished.

So be very wary of the subtle ways you shoot yourself in the foot, because they can carry over into your real efforts. If you view your biggest goals more as fantasies, then that's exactly what they'll be. And *what you think you become* (that should scare the heck out of you if you have negative, uninspired thoughts!).

Big Dreams Create Big Lessons

If you dream big your actions need to be big, your thoughts need to be big, and you'll have to be sure you don't harbor any self-doubts. Of course that takes a lot of effort, but it's also the point. If you want to change your circumstances, you're going to have to grow into a new person.

Author and motivational speaker, Jim Rohn (1930-2009), said he didn't want to become a millionaire for the money. He wanted to become a millionaire for the person he'd become in the process.

It's that way with many things. Consider the goal of becoming physically fit. In order to manifest outer strength, you have to begin with a considerable amount of inner strength. You may not have a great deal of inner strength in the beginning. But as you follow through with your goal – and gain lessons and tools along the way—you'll find the inner strength that was there all along.

A lot of people think failure and obstacles are bad things, but nothing could be further from the truth as they're part of the process! Growth is the process and resistance spurs growth. The way your muscles grow from struggling to move heavy weights against gravity is the same way every other part of you grows as well. It requires getting out of your comfort zone, trying new things, and laying claim to something that hasn't been part of your reality. If it were easy, you'd have it by now. If you do have it, you know what I mean.

Jim Rohn's philosophy was that you need to realize that the process of failure isn't the universe rejecting you, but the universe preparing you for the success you seek.

For example, let's say you want to publish a novel and you submit your manuscript to publishers and literary agents. You get negative feedback telling you what to change if you want to get it published. Of course that stings. The tempting thing to do is to ignore their advice because you've put a lot of time and effort into your script (and you think you know what you want to say better than they do).

But what you're not realizing is this is part of the process. Professional agents don't reject you for the fun of it or because they're mean-spirited; they provide re-al-world feedback that lets you know the condition of your manuscript. They've helped hundreds of people successfully get published, and supposedly know what they're doing. If you follow their advice and edit your manuscript, you stand a better chance at getting published. One day you may even look at your original manuscript and think, *Why did I ever think this was ready to publish? Man, I dodged a bullet!*

The growth you experience on your journey isn't because the path is easy; it's because the path is hard and you have a lesson to learn. The bigger you dream, the more growth you can expect to experience. And since the shortest distance between two points is a straight line, then plant your flag in your new dream and shout out to the world "I **will** have this!" and let it sort out the rest of the details.

From Dreamer to Doer

You can't just have a dream—you must become the person capable of making it happen. If you want to be a best-selling author, then you have to become that. This means writing a book that will engage people, talking to the right agents, and listening to feedback and not fighting it. Instead of trying to be a best-selling author, take on the habits and actions of a best-selling author, and eventually your reality will shift to match your energy and your actions.

Think about all the ways in which you inhabit your current reality. Your daily habits, your thoughts and your beliefs seem to match what you have. At the very least, you should be able to recognize that your perceptions match your reality; if they don't, they aren't your perceptions.

What is the importance of taking on a different inner world? If you change your inner world (your inner self), the outer world has to change to match it and there's no easy way to avoid it. The value in looking to the outer world to find success is you'll get feedback to see if your inner world has been succeeding. If it hasn't been working, you need to change your strategies.

That's why you need to make the decision at this very moment to begin inhabiting a new empowering reality that gives you confidence. You need to make the choice not only to live this reality in your perception of it, but in deeds as well.

Want to be fit? Think the thoughts a fit person would think (*I need to get to the gym or I'll blow up like a whale!*).

Want to be rich? Think the thoughts a rich person would think (*I need to get a raise or start looking for another job!*).

Want to attract a mate? Think the thoughts that will attract your perfect soul mate (*I'm going to put myself out there, and won't give up till the right one comes along!*).

Your thoughts, your actions, the words you write, the doubts you hold and the life you lead all factor into creating the reality you currently enjoy, suffer from, or lack. The choice is entirely up to you.

END OF CHAPTER ASSIGNMENT

By doing the assignments throughout this book, you should have a clearer view of what you want. You know what you want to experience, and you know the emotions and actions you can associate with your goals. You now know how to live your goals as if they are here in the present moment.

For this assignment I want you to amp up the volume on your subconscious by asking yourself if your goal has been too modest. If it has, go through each and every assignment again until you have one (or more) worthy of your time. After all, we only get a limited amount of time on this earth, so you might as well make the most of it.

If your goal is already big enough, then congratulate yourself because you have all the tools at your disposal to change your reality. But simply from the title of my book – *You Become What You Think About* – you already know your reality is under your control. What's really important is not the reality nor the circumstances you find yourself in. What really is important is you need to change what lies within you.

So what will you think about today?

BUILDING A NEW LIFE ONE THOUGHT AT A TIME

*"As a man thinketh in his heart,
so is he."*

A great deal of the world's motivational advice stems from that one simple sentence that oozes with wisdom and timeless truth.

But there's another quote I want to make you aware of: "Nothing happens until something moves." Although this one (attributed to physicist Albert Einstein) speaks to the world of physics, it could also apply to your life.

Nothing happens until something moves. If you don't change your thoughts, your actions, your beliefs, your doubts, then nothing about your circumstances will change, which is the core message of this book: the act of becoming. But you can't become what you want to be without becoming something other than what you are now.

Many people choose a rudderless life. They believe their circumstances hold all the power, and their reality reflects this belief. They float around aimlessly never finding what they're seeking, and ultimately they never make their own dreams come true. This isn't the kind of life to lead, because you never know where the currents will take you.

Instead, you should live the life of someone who knows how to steer themselves on a different course. It may not always be easy as there are often storms and gales on the horizon. But that doesn't mean your steering is pointless, because you will have learned how to manage the rudder very well. In fact, setting sail might be the most valuable thing you'll ever decide to do.

The first place you can get started is by doing all the end of chapter assignments. They're not just meant to be summaries; they're meant to galvanize you to action. This book should be considered a handbook as well as a reference guide, as it will keep you engaged in the process of "becoming."

Life is meant to be interactive. Even failures and rejections should be considered part of the "game." If you lose a game of chess, do you renounce the game altogether? Or do you keep learning the lessons and keep playing so you can become a grand master?

When building a new life your goal shouldn't be to create it all at once, because that's too much to ask of anyone. You should add small subtle thoughts one at a time that communicate to your subconscious you're already where you want to be. Over time those collective thoughts will pick up momentum—like a river that accumulates more water one raindrop at a time.

Don't think about the old way of doing things (which would be like getting in your car, putting it in reverse, and driving to your destination as you watch your house get smaller in your rearview mirror). You can't very well navigate your life like that, because in life you don't get a rearview mirror to look back—you can only look forward to the future. So you need to put your goals in front of you, and choose the straightest path to success.

- What kind of person do you need to be in order to achieve your goals?

- What kind of discipline do you need to have?

- What kind of routines should you establish?

- What kinds of thoughts should you think?

Write down your answers, and keep them somewhere prominent to keep you constantly reminded of exactly what it is you want as well as what it will take to get it. Then, inhabit your new reality like someone putting on a Halloween costume. Eventually you'll find your perceptions shifting to reflect the new reality you're wearing.

So what will your new reality be? Will it be the same one you've been living? Will it rely on your old habits and old actions? Or will your new reality be new and fresh? Will it be something you never thought you could accomplish beyond the realm of daydreams and fantasy?

You *can* accomplish your dreams, but only if you stop viewing them as fantasies. Abandon the fantasies (but keep the dreams!), take action, and start making your life what you know it can be. In time you'll see your thoughts truly did get you where you want to be. And that is a powerful realization, because it puts you in the driver's seat of your own life.

You become what you think about! So don't you think it's time to change your thoughts to match your dreams?

For a free book of Napoleon Hill's classic *Think and Grow Rich,* go to: Get-My-Free-Book.net

ABOUT THE AUTHOR

Twelve years ago Vic Johnson was totally unknown in the personal development field. Since that time he's created six of the most popular personal development sites on the Internet. One of them, www.AsA-Manthinketh.net has given away over 400,000 copies of James Allen's classic book. Three of them are listed in the top 5% of websites in the world (English language).

This success came despite the fact that he and his family were evicted from their home 16 years ago and the next year his last automobile was repossessed. His story of redemption and victory has inspired thousands around the world as he has taught the powerful principles that created incredible wealth in his life and for many others.

Today he serves more than 300,000 subscribers from virtually every country in the world. He's become an internationally known expert in goal-achieving, and has hosted his own TV show, *Goals 2 Go*, on TSTN.

His book, *13 Secrets of World Class Achievers,* is the number one goal-setting book at both the Kindle store and Apple iBookstore.

Another best seller, *Day by Day with James Allen,* has sold more than 75,000 copies and has been translated into Japanese, Czech, Slovak and Farsi.

Vic's three-day weekend seminar event, *Claim Your Power Now,* has attracted such icons as Bob Proctor, Jim Rohn, Denis Waitley and many others.

His websites include:

AsAManThinketh.net

Goals2Go.com

GettingRichWitheBooks.com

TheChampionsClub.org

MyDailyInsights.com

VicJohnson.com

ClaimYourPowerNow.com

LaurenzanaPress.com

OTHER BOOKS BY VIC JOHNSON

Day by Day with James Allen

How To Write A Book This Weekend, Even If You Flunked English Like I Did

Goal Setting: 13 Secrets of World Class Achievers

It's Never Too Late And You're Never Too Old : 50 People Who Found Success After 50

52 Mondays: The One Year Path To Outrageous Success & Lifelong Happiness

The Magic of Believing: Believe in Yourself and The Universe Is Forced to Believe In You

Self Help Books: The 101 Best Personal Development

How I Created a Six Figure Income Giving Away a Dead Guy's Book

Think and Grow Rich: The Lost Secret

50 Lessons I Learned From The World's #1 Goal Achiever

How To Make Extra Money: 100 Perfect Businesses for Part-Time and Retirement Income

Made in United States
Orlando, FL
09 December 2024

55217840R00075